P9-CBM-491

TEAM SPIRIT ®

SMART BOOKS FOR YOUNG FANS

THE BOSTON BRUINS

BY

MARK STEWART

CONTENT CONSULTANT
DENIS GIBBONS
SOCIETY FOR INTERNATIONAL HOCKEY RESEARCH

NORWOOD HOUSE PRESS

CHICAGO, ILLINOIS

Norwood House Press
P.O. Box 316598
Chicago, Illinois 60631

For information regarding Norwood House Press, please visit our website at:
www.norwoodhousepress.com or call 866-565-2900.

All photos courtesy of Associated Press except the following:
McDiarmid/Cartophilium (6, 34 left), Goudey Gum Co. (7, 42 bottom),
Getty Images (8, 12, 25, 32, 35 bottom), Topps, Inc. (9, 15, 22), Esso/Imperial Oil Ltd. (10),
The Sporting News (18), Parkhurst Products (21), Beckett Publications (23), Dodd, Mead and Company (28),
Author's Collection (33, 37), Boy Scouts of America (34 right), Black Book Partners (35 top, 40, 41, 43),
Imperial Tobacco (39), Parade Sportive (42 top), Bee Hive Golden Corn Syrup/Cargill, Inc. (45).
Cover Photo: AP Photo/Mike Carlson

The memorabilia and artifacts pictured in this book are presented for educational and informational purposes,
and come from the collection of the author.

Editor: Mike Kennedy
Designer: Ron Jaffe
Project Management: Black Book Partners, LLC.
Special thanks to Topps, Inc.

Library of Congress Cataloging-in-Publication Data

Stewart, Mark, 1960 July 7-
    The Boston Bruins / by Mark Stewart. -- Revised edition.
        pages cm. -- (Team spirit)
    Includes bibliographical references and index.
    Summary: "A revised Team Spirit Hockey edition featuring the Boston Bruins
that chronicles the history and accomplishments of the team. Includes access
to the Team Spirit website which provides additional information and
photos"-- Provided by publisher.

    ISBN 978-1-59953-616-3 (library edition : alk. paper) -- ISBN
978-1-60357-624-6 (ebook) 1. Boston Bruins (Hockey
team)--History--Juvenile literature. 2. Hockey--United States--Juvenile
literature. I. Title.
    GV848.B6S74 2014
    796.962'640974461--dc23
                                        2013034577

Manufactured in the United States of America in Stevens Point, Wisconsin.
239N—012014

COVER PHOTO: The Bruins show team spirit after a goal during the 2012–13 season.

TABLE OF CONTENTS

ABOUT OUR GLOSSARY

In this book, there may be several words that you are reading for the first time. Some are sports words, some are new vocabulary words, and some are familiar words that are used in an unusual way. All of these words are defined on page 46. Throughout the book, sports words appear in **bold type**. Regular vocabulary words appear in ***bold italic type***.

MEET THE BRUINS

Brown bears may look warm and cuddly, but they can be unpredictable and dangerous. The same could be said of the Boston Bruins—a "bruin" is another name for a brown bear. The Bruins are known for striking quickly and with great *ferocity*. This has helped them win the **Stanley Cup** six times.

The Bruins like to build around players with unusual talents. Sometimes that player is a superstar who can control the game all by himself. Sometimes he is a role player who finds amazing ways to make his teammates better. The people who run the Bruins know just where to locate these players. They are good at finding talent where others fail to look.

This book tells the story of the Bruins. They win games by mixing strong defense with powerful skating and shooting. They win championships when they have a dressing room full of *dynamic* players. They win fans by playing hard and never giving up.

Brad Marchand and Patrice Bergeron offers words of encouragement to Tyler Seguin during the 2012–13 season.

GLORY DAYS

In the early 1920s, the **National Hockey League (NHL)** was only "national" in Canada. No NHL team was located in the United States. That changed in 1924, when the Boston Bruins joined the league. The NHL soon had an entire American **Division**, which also included teams in Chicago, Pittsburgh, Detroit, and New York.

Boston won only six games in its first season. However, by the end of the *decade*, the Bruins were one of the top NHL teams. They reached the **Stanley Cup Finals** three times in four years and won the championship once. Boston's stars included Cooney Weiland, Dit Clapper, Harry Oliver, Lionel Hitchman, and Cecil "Tiny" Thompson.

The player who made the Bruins roar was Eddie Shore. Boston fans loved him. Shore was a violent and aggressive defensive player who loved to *ambush* opponents by charging toward the net from his position on defense. Most defensemen at this time preferred to conserve their energy and stay back to protect their own goal.

SPORT KINGS GUM

EDDIE SHORE

How popular was Shore? After warm-ups in Boston Garden, he would remain on the ice, wait for the lights to go dark, and then skate into the spotlight. The organist would play "Hail to the Chief"— the same song played for the President of the United States!

Shore led the Bruins to their second Stanley Cup in 1939. The team continued to win after he retired the following year. Boston captured its third Stanley Cup in 1941. That club was led by Milt Schmidt, Woody Dumart, and Bobby Bauer. Other stars included goalie Frank Brimsek, playmaker Bill Cowley, and Roy Conacher, who topped the NHL in scoring as a **rookie**.

During the 1950s and 1960s, the Bruins put more fine players on the ice. One of their best was a rugged defenseman named Fern Flaman. Three others—Johnny Bucyk, Vic Stasiuk, and Rudy "Bronco" Horvath—formed the high-scoring "Uke **Line**." The trio earned that nickname because all were from Ukraine. They helped the Bruins reach the Stanley Cup Finals in 1958.

LEFT: Cecil "Tiny" Thompson always stood tall in goal for the Bruins.
ABOVE: No player was more popular with Boston fans than Eddie Shore.

In 1966, a young defenseman named Bobby Orr joined the team. Orr was a superstar from the moment he began his NHL career. He was a lightning-fast skater who seemed to know what teammates and opponents would do before they did it. No one had seen a player like Orr before. Not long after he arrived, the Bruins made a great trade for Phil Esposito, Ken Hodge, and Fred Stanfield. They turned a good team into a great one.

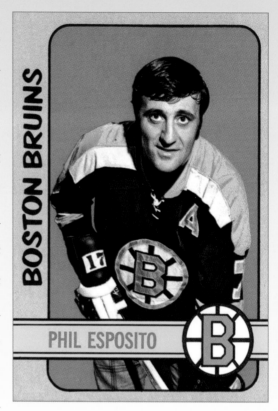

Starting in 1967–68, Boston reached the **playoffs** each season for 29 years in a row. Orr became the first defenseman to top 100 points (goals plus **assists**) in a season. Esposito set an NHL record with 76 goals in 1970–71. They teamed up with Wayne Cashman, Ed Westfall, Derek Sanderson, Dallas Smith, and goalie Gerry Cheevers to give the Bruins great balance on offense and defense. Boston reached the Stanley Cup Finals five times during the 1970s and won the championship twice.

In the 1980s, the Bruins welcomed a new group of leaders. Terry O'Reilly, Rick Middleton, Barry Pederson, Pete Peeters,

LEFT: Bobby Orr skates across center ice with the puck.
ABOVE: Phil Esposito was known to Boston fans as "Espo."

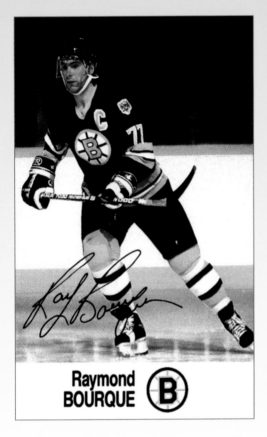

Raymond
BOURQUE (B)

Peter McNab, Cam Neely, and Ray Bourque ranked among the top players in the NHL. Bourque stood out as an all-time great. He reminded many fans around the league of Orr.

Bourque helped the Bruins reach the Stanley Cup Finals in 1988, and once again in 1990. In both seasons, Boston defeated the Montreal Canadiens in the playoffs. It was a sweet feeling because of the heated rivalry between the teams. Still, beating the Canadiens did not replace the thrill of winning another Stanley Cup. Boston fans ached to see the Bruins hold the trophy high once again.

In 1996–97, the Bruins missed the playoffs for the first time since the 1960s. Boston began rebuilding around talented new players such as Joe Thornton, Jason Allison, and Sergei Samsonov. They helped the team return to its winning ways, but Boston did not make it back to the Stanley Cup Finals.

When the Bruins began trading these stars and rebuilding the team again, many fans thought it was a mistake—especially after Thornton won the Hart Trophy as the league's **Most Valuable Player (MVP)**

with the San Jose Sharks. Meanwhile, the other major sports teams in New England all won championships. The Bruins were under pressure to do the same.

In 2008–09, Boston rediscovered the winning *formula*. Coach Claude Julien mixed **veterans** Zdeno Chara, Tim Thomas, Nathan Horton, Dennis Seidenberg, Michael Ryder, and Mark Recchi with young players such as David Krejci, Milan Lucic, Brad Marchand, and Patrice Bergeron. At season's end, Boston had the best record in its **conference**. In 2010–11, the long wait finally ended. Boston returned to the Stanley Cup Finals and defeated the Vancouver Canucks in seven games for the team's sixth NHL championship.

LEFT: Ray Bourque followed in the footsteps of Bobby Orr.
ABOVE: Tim Thomas and David Krejci embrace during Boston's run to its sixth Stanley Cup.

HOME ICE

For most of their time in the NHL, the Bruins played their home games in Boston Garden. The arena was built for boxing matches. For hockey games, this meant that many seats were close to the ice and fans got amazing close-up views of the action. This was tough on visiting players. So was the fact that the rink itself was several feet shorter than others in the NHL.

In 1995, the Bruins moved into a new arena that fans still call "The Garden." Like the old building, it sits atop Boston's North Station. Fans can reach the arena by train or bus from almost anywhere in Massachusetts. Many simply walk to games from surrounding neighborhoods.

BY THE NUMBERS

- *The team's arena has 17,565 seats for hockey.*
- *The "old" Garden and "new" Garden were built only nine inches apart.*
- *As of 2013–14, the Bruins have retired 10 numbers: 2 (Eddie Shore), 3 (Lionel Hitchman), 4 (Bobby Orr), 5 (Dit Clapper), 7 (Phil Esposito), 8 (Cam Neely), 9 (Johnny Bucyk), 15 (Milt Schmidt), 24 (Terry O'Reilly), and 77 (Ray Bourque).*

Banners from the Bruins' championship seasons and retired numbers of famous players hang from the ceiling of the team's arena.

Boston's first official colors were brown and gold. They meant a lot to team owner Charles Adams. He also used them in his grocery store chain, Finast Foods. Boston switched to black and gold during the 1930s. Also during that decade, the Bruins began using a large *B* on the front of their uniforms. In the 1940s, a circle was added around this ***logo***. The team has made several small changes to its uniform since then.

When the Bruins play at home, they usually wear a black sweater with black sleeves and gold around the shoulders. On the road, the players often wear a white sweater. Sometimes the Bruins wear a special black road uniform. It shows a bear and also has the name of the team and city on the front.

ALL-TIME GREATS

DIT CLAPPER

LEFT: Brad Marchand wears the Boston away uniform during the 2012–13 season.   **ABOVE**: This trading card of Dit Clapper shows the team uniform when Boston used brown instead of black.

WE WON!

Every championship in hockey takes a team effort. That has been especially true for the Bruins. Each time they lifted the Stanley Cup, it was the result of hard work and unselfish play. In 1929, the Bruins beat the New York Rangers in a best-of-three series. Their star was rookie goalie Tiny Thompson. He stopped all but one of the shots New York fired at him. With the young netminder playing like a veteran, the Bruins won two close games on goals by Dit Clapper and Bill Carson.

Ten years later, the Bruins returned to the top of the NHL. They beat the Rangers in the opening round of the playoffs, but some New York fans are still wondering how. The Rangers were in control of six of the seven games. The difference for Boston was Mel Hill, who ended three games with goals in **overtime**. The exhausted Bruins went on to beat the Toronto Maple Leafs in the finals in five games.

The Bruins had an easier time in 1941, when they defeated the Detroit Red Wings for the Stanley Cup. The Red Wings decided to play fast, wide-open hockey, thinking they could out-hustle the

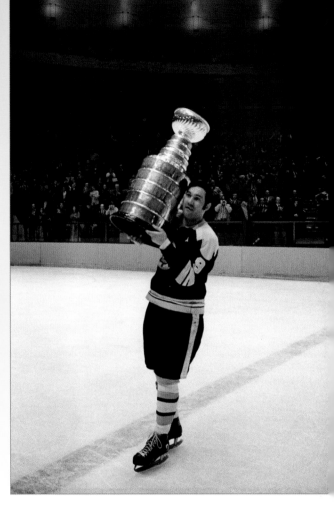

Johnny Bucyk shows off the Stanley Cup to Boston fans in 1970.

Boston players. That was a mistake. The Bruins loved that style of play. Each contest was close, but Boston won four in a row. Milt Schmidt and Roy Conacher each broke a tie with a game-winning goal.

The next time the Bruins raised the Stanley Cup was at the end of the 1969–70 season. The NHL had grown to a dozen teams. Boston had the game's best player, Bobby Orr. He led a powerful offense that included Phil Esposito, John McKenzie, Johnny Bucyk, and Derek Sanderson. The Bruins skated against the St. Louis Blues in the Stanley Cup Finals. Scotty Bowman, the coach of the Blues, knew his team faced a stiff challenge. "We practiced covering Bobby Orr for six hours today," Bowman joked at one point. "But the only trouble is, we don't have a Bobby Orr to practice against!"

1972-73 PRO AND AMATEUR

HOCKEY GUIDE

PUBLISHED BY
The Sporting News

The Bruins won the first three games easily. When the final game of the series went into overtime, everyone expected Orr to make the winning play. He came through with the championship goal to complete a four-game sweep of the Blues. Orr was the star again when Boston won its fifth Stanley Cup, in 1972, against the Rangers. Gerry Cheevers also had a tremendous series.

At this point, no one in Boston imagined that it would take another 39 years before the Bruins lifted the Stanley Cup again. But the team did not win its next NHL crown until 2011. Center David Krejci and defenseman Zdeno Chara led Boston into the playoffs, where the club survived close calls against the Montreal Canadiens and the Tampa Bay Lightning. Playing in the Stanley Cup Finals for the first time since 1992, the Bruins faced the Vancouver Canucks. Veteran goalie Tim Thomas had played brilliantly throughout the playoffs. Now the fans were counting on him to stop the high-scoring Canucks in the championship round.

Thomas allowed only six goals in the first five games, but the Bruins still found themselves behind in the series. In the first period of Game 6, Boston scored four goals in less than five minutes and went on to win 5–2. The seventh and deciding game was played in Vancouver, where the Canucks could be very tough. On this night, however, Thomas was even tougher. He turned back all 37 shots he faced. Patrice Bergeron and Brad Marchand each scored twice. The Bruins won the game 4–0 and celebrated the team's sixth Stanley Cup.

LEFT: The front of the 1972–73 *Sporting News Hockey Guide* shows the championship duo of Bobby Orr and Gerry Cheevers.   **ABOVE**: The Bruins pose with the Stanley Cup in 2011.

GO-TO GUYS

T o be a true star in the NHL, you need more than a great slapshot. You have to be a "go-to guy"—someone teammates trust to make the winning play when the seconds are ticking away in a big game. Bruins fans have had a lot to cheer about over the years, including these great stars …

THE PIONEERS

LIONEL HITCHMAN   Defenseman

• BORN: 11/3/1901 • DIED: 12/19/1968 • PLAYED FOR TEAM: 1924–25 TO 1933–34

As a defenseman, Lionel Hitchman was like a brick wall. This let teammate Eddie Shore rush the net on offense. Hitchman and Shore played together for seven seasons and were considered the greatest defensive pair of their time. Hitchman was named team captain in 1928–29 and led the Bruins to the Stanley Cup that season.

EDDIE SHORE   Defenseman

• BORN: 11/25/1902 • DIED: 3/16/1985 • PLAYED FOR TEAM: 1926–27 TO 1939–40

Eddie Shore had the speed and skill of a forward, but he was tough enough to be a defenseman. This made him hockey's best "two-way" player. Shore paid a price for his aggressiveness—he needed more than 900 stitches during his career to close his many wounds.

DIT CLAPPER   Right Wing/Defenseman

• BORN: 2/9/1907 • DIED: 1/21/1978 • PLAYED FOR TEAM: 1927–28 TO 1946–47

Dit Clapper was a star in Boston for a long time. In fact, the NHL put him in the **Hall of Fame** the night he retired. Clapper was the first player to wear the same team's uniform for 20 seasons.

TINY THOMPSON   Goalie

• BORN: 5/31/1905 • DIED: 2/9/1981 • PLAYED FOR TEAM: 1928–29 TO 1938–39

Cecil Thompson got his nickname as a joke during his youth hockey days. He was actually the tallest player on his team! Thompson won the Vezina Trophy as the NHL's top goalie four times.

MILT SCHMIDT   Center

• BORN: 3/5/1918

• PLAYED FOR TEAM: 1936–37 TO 1954–55

Milt Schmidt always found a way to make his teammates better. In 1950–51, the Bruins had a losing record. But Schmidt was so good that he was awarded the Hart Trophy as the league MVP.

FRANK BRIMSEK   Goalie

• BORN: 9/26/1915 • DIED: 11/11/1998 • PLAYED FOR TEAM: 1938–39 TO 1948–49

Frank Brimsek recorded a **shutout** in six of his first eight NHL games. The rest of his rookie season went even better. "Mr. Zero" won the Vezina Trophy and the Calder Trophy as the league's best rookie—and then led the Bruins to the Stanley Cup.

ABOVE: Milt Schmidt

BOBBY ORR
Defenseman

• BORN: 3/20/1948   • PLAYED FOR TEAM: 1966–67 TO 1975–76

Bobby Orr turned the Bruins from a losing team into an NHL powerhouse. In the process, he changed the game of hockey, setting the stage for all the fast-skating defensemen who followed him. In 1970–71, Orr had a record-setting **plus/minus rating** of +124.

PHIL ESPOSITO
Center

• BORN: 2/20/1942   • PLAYED FOR TEAM: 1967–68 TO 1975–76

A big body and lightning-quick reflexes made Phil Esposito impossible to stop when he found a spot near the net. Espo topped 100 points five years in a row. He won the Hart Trophy twice during his nine seasons as a Bruin.

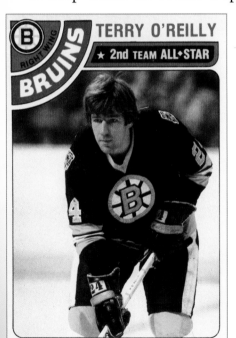

TERRY O'REILLY
Right Wing

• BORN: 6/7/1961

• PLAYED FOR TEAM: 1971–72 TO 1984–85

Terry O'Reilly's job was to protect Boston's high-scoring stars. He did so with such force and energy that teammates called him "Taz"—short for Tasmanian Devil. O'Reilly was a good scorer and excellent defensive player. In 1987–88, he coached the team to the Stanley Cup Finals.

RAY BOURQUE   Defenseman

- BORN 12/28/1960   • PLAYED FOR TEAM: 1979–80 TO 1999–2000

Ray Bourque used his terrific skating and shooting to control the pace of the game. As a rookie, Bourque was the first player at his position ever to win the Calder Trophy and earn recognition as a **First-Team All-Star**. He also won the Norris Trophy as the NHL's top defenseman five times.

CAM NEELY   Right Wing

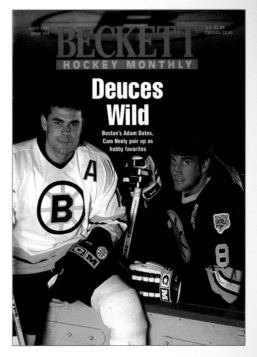

- BORN: 6/6/1965
- PLAYED FOR TEAM: 1986–87 TO 1995–96

Cam Neely was one of the scariest players in hockey. He had a hard, accurate shot and a short temper. Plus, no one ever outworked him. Neely had a great scoring touch and formed a dangerous duo with linemate Adam Oates.

ZDENO CHARA   Defenseman

- BORN: 3/18/1977   • FIRST SEASON WITH TEAM: 2006–07

In the early years of the NHL, no one could have imagined a player like Zdeno Chara. When the Bruins signed him, he was the tallest player in league history at 6′ 9″. Chara moved with great *agility* and had the NHL's hardest slapshot. In 2011, he captained Boston to the Stanley Cup.

LEFT: Terry O'Reilly
ABOVE: Adam Oates and Cam Neely

CALLING THE SHOTS

Few teams in any sport can claim as many legendary coaches as the Bruins. Their first coach, Art Ross, actually named the team—and then oversaw three Stanley Cup championships from behind the bench and as a team *executive*. As if that weren't enough, the NHL scoring trophy was named in his honor. Superstars Cy Denneny and Cooney Weiland also guided the Bruins to the Stanley Cup in the team's early years. Other former players who led the Bruins to glory were Dit Clapper and Milt Schmidt.

In 1966–67, the Bruins were the youngest team in the NHL. That included their coach, Harry Sinden. Three seasons later, Sinden guided the team to its fourth Stanley Cup. He left the Bruins and coached Team Canada in a 1972 series against the Soviet Union. Sinden later returned to Boston to run the team's business affairs.

Tom Johnson led the Bruins to their fifth Stanley Cup in 1972. He was followed by other top coaches, including Don Cherry and Pat Burns. Both won the Jack Adams Award as the NHL's top coach. Although Cherry did not win a championship, he probably rates as Boston's most popular leader. After Boston traded

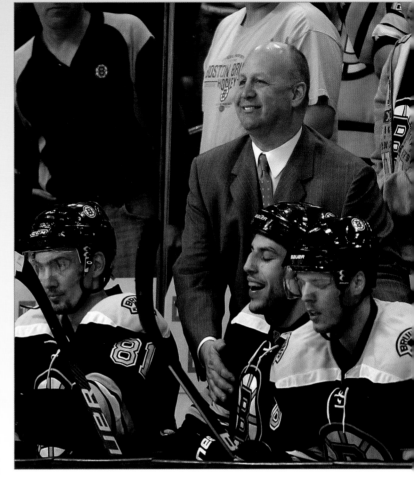

Claude Julien shares a laugh with one of his players on the bench.

away many of its scoring stars (including Bobby Orr and Phil Esposito), Cherry remade the team as a physical club that came to be known as the "Big Bad Bruins." They finished in first place in their division four years in a row and got contributions from every player on the squad. In 1977–78, 11 different players scored 20 or more goals!

In 2008–09, Claude Julien led the Bruins to 53 victories and a division championship. He became the team's third Jack Adams Award winner. One year later, Julien nearly lost his job when the Bruins fell to the Philadelphia Flyers in the playoffs. But the Bruins smartly kept him behind the bench, and he led them to their sixth Stanley Cup in 2011.

ONE GREAT DAY

From the day Bobby Orr joined the Bruins in 1966, their fans dared to dream of winning the Stanley Cup. For nearly two decades before Orr came along, the team struggled to win more games than it lost each season. But by the time the 1970 playoffs began, the Bruins and their fans felt the team was unbeatable. Boston defeated the New York Rangers in a rowdy series and then swept the Chicago Blackhawks in four games. The only team left between the Bruins and the Stanley Cup was the St. Louis Blues.

Orr was the NHL's scoring champ in 1969–70, with 120 points. No defenseman had ever claimed that honor before. Right behind him, in second place in scoring, was Phil Esposito. Together, they helped Boston cruise to victories in the first three games against the Blues.

Game 4 was a different matter. The Bruins attacked the St. Louis net all game. They scored three times, but the Blues netted three goals of their own. The game went into overtime. Boston fans barely had time to settle back into their seats when Orr streaked toward the

Bobby Orr, arms raised, flies through the air after his goal
that won the 1970 Stanley Cup.

St. Louis net. He passed to Derek Sanderson and then glided to the
goal. Sanderson slid the puck back to Orr, who whacked it past goalie
Glenn Hall. The Bruins won 4–3 and celebrated their first Stanley
Cup since 1941.

Orr was tripped as he fired the shot that produced the game-
winning goal. In fact, he was still in midair when the goal light
flashed on, and he raised his arms in celebration. Orr had already
won the Norris Trophy, Hart Trophy, and **Art Ross Trophy**. His
amazing goal guaranteed a fourth award—the Conn Smythe Trophy
as MVP of the playoffs.

LEGEND HAS IT

WHO WAS THE MOST SURPRISED BRUIN IN 1971?

I've Got To Be Me

by Derek Sanderson
with Stan Fischler

LEGEND HAS IT that Derek Sanderson was. Sanderson was one of hockey's most handsome *bachelors*. He even did some fashion modeling. So when the team held a "Win a Date with Derek" contest during the 1970–71 season, it came as no shock when more than 10,000 entries rolled in. Sanderson could hardly wait to meet the winner. His teammates got a good laugh when the winning entry came from a 72-year-old with 12 grandchildren.

ABOVE: Being Derek Sanderson meant getting plenty of dates … and a big surprise in 1971!

DID THE BRUINS ISSUE THE MOST UNFAIR PLAYER FINE IN HISTORY?

LEGEND HAS IT that they did. In 1929, Boston's star player, Eddie Shore, got caught in traffic and missed the team train to Montreal. He drove 350 miles, through the mountains, during an ice storm, and arrived just in time for the game. Shore played all 60 minutes and scored the only goal in a 1–0 victory. The team fined him $500 anyway.

WHO WAS THE NHL'S "STREAKIEST" GOALIE?

LEGEND HAS IT that Gerry Cheevers was. But not all Boston fans agree. During one stretch in the 1971–72 season, Cheevers set an NHL record with a 32-game unbeaten streak. In all, he won 24 games and recorded eight more ties without a loss. In 1975–76, Gilles Gilbert won 17 games in a row for the Bruins. Whose streak is the best? Fans are still arguing about that one.

Of all the cool nicknames you could have, "Sudden Death" probably might not be anyone's first choice. But Mel Hill made it work. When the 1938–39 season began, Hill was unknown to most NHL fans, even in Boston. He was just another young player trying to earn ice time. By the end of the season, however, he was practically a household name.

Hill scored 10 goals that year and helped the Bruins finish with the best record in the NHL. Still, he was just a "spare part" when the Bruins faced the New York Rangers in the playoffs. The Bruins had a strong team, and everyone expected them to capture the Stanley Cup without much of a problem.

The Rangers put up a great fight. In Game 1, the score was tied 1–1 after 60 minutes. Two overtime periods passed without either team scoring. Finally, in the third overtime, Bill Cowley passed to Hill, who lifted a shot into the net to win the game. Two nights later, the Bruins and Rangers were tied 2–2 after three periods. Once again, Hill ended the game with an overtime goal. The Rangers would not quit. They won three of the next four games to

Sudden Death Hill scrambles on the ice for a loose puck in the 1940–41 Stanley Cup Finals. He had earned his nickname two years earlier.

set up an exciting Game 7. No one was surprised when neither club could break a 1–1 tie.

In the third overtime, Cowley controlled the puck behind the New York net and saw Hill open at the mouth of the goal. Cowley put a pass right on his stick. Hill flipped the puck over the goalie to win the series—and the Bruins went on to capture the Stanley Cup. From that day on, he was known as Sudden Death Hill.

"I was a basic, *unspectacular* player who usually performed well when it counted," Hill said. "I just happened to get super-hot in that series with New York."

TEAM SPIRIT

How good are Bruins fans? Wicked good! They know their players and their team history, and they understand hockey. They make Boston's home ice truly feel like home. And they can make visiting players very uncomfortable.

The Bruins have many *traditions*—and the team keeps adding to them. In 2010, Boston beat the Philadelphia Flyers in an outdoor game at baseball's Fenway Park called the Winter Classic. Patrice Bergeron and Marco Sturm teamed up to win the game in overtime. Afterwards, the Bruins raised their sticks together to salute the fans.

The team *mascot* is Blades the Bruin. Blades was named by Jillian Dempsey, who was a big fan of the Bruins as a kid. She grew up to be a star hockey player for nearby Harvard University. Blades shares the arena with the Ice Girls, the Bruins' dance team.

LEFT: The Bruins acknowledge their fans after the 2010 Winter Classic.
ABOVE: Fans wore this pin during Boston's trip to the Stanley Cup Finals in 1990.

TIMELINE

The hockey season is played from October through June. That means each season takes place at the end of one year and the beginning of the next. In this timeline, the accomplishments of the Bruins are shown by season.

1928–29
The Bruins win their first Stanley Cup.

1959–60
Bronco Horvath ties for the NHL lead in goals.

1924–25
Boston becomes the first U.S. city in the NHL.

1939–40
Three Bruins finish 1–2–3 in the NHL scoring race.

1966–67
Bobby Orr wins the Calder Trophy.

Cooney Weiland starred for the 1929 champs.

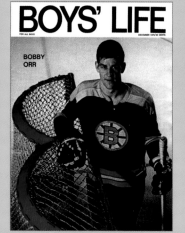

BOYS' LIFE

BOBBY ORR

Bobby Orr

Cam
Neely

1973–74
The Bruins have the top four scorers in the NHL.

1993–94
Cam Neely scores 50 goals in 49 games.

2010–11
The Bruins win their sixth Stanley Cup.

1971–72
Boston wins the Stanley Cup for the second time in three seasons.

1982–83
Pete Peeters wins the Vezina Trophy.

2008–09
Zdeno Chara sets a record with a 105.4 mph (169.62 kph) slapshot.

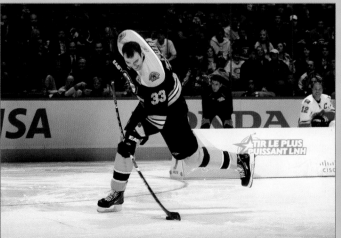

Zdeno
Chara

FUN FACTS

IRON MAN

In 1963–64, Eddie Johnston played every minute of all 70 games for the Bruins. The super-tough goalie broke his nose several times—and twice doctors had to use *leeches* to drain blood from his eyes so that he could see!

SHORE THING

In 1928, the New York Rangers offered defenseman Myles Lane to the Bruins in exchange for Eddie Shore. Owner Jack Adams responded, "You are so many Myles from Shore that you need a life preserver."

THE TANK

Goalie Tim Thomas was nicknamed "The Tank" for his fearless style. In 2010–11, he had one of the best seasons in NHL history. That year, Thomas became just the second goalie in league history to lead his team to the Stanley Cup while winning the Vezina Trophy and the Conn Smythe Trophy.

RIGHT: Joe Thornton

LONG TIME COMING

In 1999–2000, Joe Thornton led Boston in goals, assists, and penalty minutes. The last Bruin to do that was Jimmy Herberts—75 seasons earlier!

IN STITCHES

The first NHL goalie to decorate his mask was Gerry Cheevers. He painted "Frankenstein stitches" over

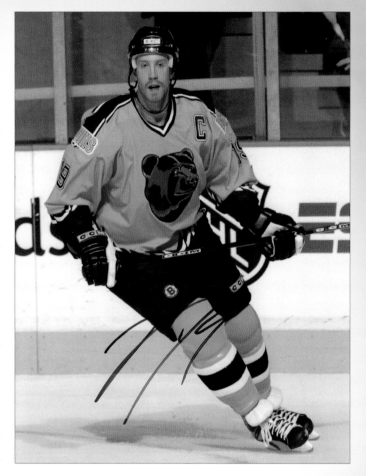

the spots where pucks would have cut his face. Cheevers filled up four masks before his career was over!

BREAKING BARRIERS

On January 18, 1958, the Bruins called up Willie O'Ree from the **minor leagues**. When he took the ice against the Montreal Canadiens that night, he became the first black player in NHL history. In 2008, the NHL celebrated the 50th anniversary of that moment in Boston and later at the **All-Star Game**.

TALKING HOCKEY

"This is what every kid dreams of—scoring the winning goal in a Stanley Cup overtime final. Wow!"

► **BOBBY ORR**, *on his goal against the St. Louis Blues in 1970*

"It meant as much to me to give a big hit as it did to score a big goal. And to leave a mark for being that kind of player is special to me."

► **CAM NEELY**, *on his ability the deliver hard body blows*

"I was a lucky guy … I don't care what anyone says. You can't do it alone. It takes a good team for you to be a good player."

► **PHIL ESPOSITO**, *on the teamwork that helped him set a new goal-scoring record*

"Never make a move until the man with the puck makes his. There's no room for guesswork in goaltending."

► **TINY THOMPSON**, *on the key to making one-on-one saves*

"The kid had the fastest hands I ever saw."

▶ **ART ROSS**, *on goalie Frank Brimsek*

"There was no better person than Bobby ... He was the brains of the line—always thinking, and a very clever playmaker."

▶ **WOODY DUMART**, *on his linemate, Bobby Bauer*

"I contributed physically and stayed out of the penalty box."

▶ **JOHNNY BUCYK**, *on how he twice won the Lady Byng Trophy for good sportsmanship*

ART ROSS OF HAILEYBURY CLUB

"I enjoy the job. I enjoy being around players. I enjoy the whole process, just not the ***limelight*** that comes with it."

▶ **CLAUDE JULIEN**, *on the pressure of coaching the Bruins*

"Our family thought if you could be unselfish, your teammates would always like you."

▶ **ADAM OATES**, *on what he learned about hockey from watching soccer with his father*

ABOVE: Art Ross

GREAT DEBATES

People who root for the Bruins love to compare their favorite moments, teams, and players. Some debates have been going on for years! How would you settle these classic hockey arguments?

THE TRADE FOR CAM NEELY WAS THE BEST IN TEAM HISTORY ...

... because the Bruins got a Hall of Famer for next to nothing. The Vancouver Canucks thought Neely was a poor defensive player, so they traded him—along with a first-round pick in the NHL **draft**—for Barry Pederson, who was injured at the time. Pederson had a couple of good years in Vancouver, but Neely became one of the NHL's top scorers. In 1993–94, he scored 50 goals in 49 games!

THE 1967 TRADE WITH THE CHICAGO BLACKHAWKS WAS THE BEST EVER ...

... because it helped the Bruins win two Stanley Cups. Chicago traded Phil Esposito, Ken Hodge (LEFT), and Fred Stanfield to Boston. The Bruins gave up three good players, but none came close to matching the production of Esposito, Hodge, and Stanfield. Chicago fans are still angry about this trade. They believe that their Blackhawks could have become a *dynasty* if the team had turned down the trade.

GERRY CHEEVERS WAS THE BRUINS' GREATEST GOALIE ...

... because he led them to two Stanley Cups in three years. Cheevers (RIGHT) was just as good in the regular season. He finished among the top five goalies in victories five years in a row. Cheevers confounded opponents by flopping to the ice to cover the entire goal line. He also liked to stray far from the net to cut down a shooter's angle—he was almost a third defenseman at times.

HELLO? YOU CAN'T GET ANY BETTER THAN FRANK BRIMSEK ...

... because his nickname was Mr. Zero! He had 10 shutouts in 43 games during his rookie season and led the team to the championship. Brimsek won a second Stanley Cup two years later and also earned the Vezina Trophy twice during his career. Mr. Zero finished with 35 shutouts in nine seasons with Boston.

The great Bruins teams and players have left their marks on the record books. These are the "best of the best" …

PARADE SPORTIVE
PAUL STUART
LE PREMIER PROGRAMME DU GENRE

Bill COWLEY

Bill Cowley

EDDIE SHORE
BOSTON "BRUINS" - Defense

Eddie Shore

BRUINS AWARD WINNERS

VEZINA TROPHY
TOP GOALTENDER

Tiny Thompson	1929–30
Tiny Thompson	1932–33
Tiny Thompson	1935–36
Tiny Thompson	1937–38
Frank Brimsek	1938–39
Frank Brimsek	1941–42
Pete Peeters	1982–83
Tim Thomas	2008–09
Tim Thomas	2010–11

JAMES NORRIS MEMORIAL TROPHY
TOP DEFENSEMAN

Bobby Orr	1967–68
Bobby Orr	1968–69
Bobby Orr	1969–70
Bobby Orr	1970–71
Bobby Orr	1971–72
Bobby Orr	1972–73
Bobby Orr	1973–74
Bobby Orr	1974–75
Ray Bourque	1986–87
Ray Bourque	1987–88
Ray Bourque	1989–90
Ray Bourque	1990–91
Ray Bourque	1993–94
Zdeno Chara	2008–09

CONN SMYTHE TROPHY
MVP DURING PLAYOFFS

Bobby Orr	1969–70
Bobby Orr	1971–72
Tim Thomas	2010–11

CALDER TROPHY
TOP ROOKIE

Frank Brimsek	1938–39
Jack Gelineau	1949–50
Larry Regan	1956–57
Bobby Orr	1966–67
Derek Sanderson	1967–68
Ray Bourque	1979–80
Sergei Samsonov	1997–98
Andrew Raycroft	2003–04

ART ROSS TROPHY
TOP SCORER

Phil Esposito	1968–69
Bobby Orr	1969–70
Phil Esposito	1970–71
Phil Esposito	1971–72
Phil Esposito	1972–73
Phil Esposito	1973–74
Bobby Orr	1974–75

HART MEMORIAL TROPHY
MOST VALUABLE PLAYER

Eddie Shore	1932–33
Eddie Shore	1934–35
Eddie Shore	1935–36
Eddie Shore	1937–38
Bill Cowley	1940–41
Bill Cowley	1942–43
Milt Schmidt	1950–51
Phil Esposito	1968–69
Bobby Orr	1969–70
Bobby Orr	1970–71
Bobby Orr	1971–72
Phil Esposito	1973–74

BRUINS ACHIEVEMENTS

ACHIEVEMENT	YEAR
Stanley Cup Finalists	1926–27
Stanley Cup Champions	1928–29
Stanley Cup Finalists	1929–30
Stanley Cup Champions	1938–39
Stanley Cup Champions	1940–41
Stanley Cup Finalists	1942–43
Stanley Cup Finalists	1945–46
Stanley Cup Finalists	1952–53
Stanley Cup Finalists	1956–57
Stanley Cup Finalists	1957–58
Stanley Cup Champions	1969–70
Stanley Cup Champions	1971–72
Stanley Cup Finalists	1973–74
Stanley Cup Finalists	1976–77
Stanley Cup Finalists	1977–78
Stanley Cup Finalists	1987–88
Stanley Cup Finalists	1989–90
Stanley Cup Champions	2010–11
Stanley Cup Finalists	2012–13

ABOVE: Ed Westfall was a key player for the 1970 champs and the 1972 champs.
BELOW: Phil Esposito fires a shot from in front of the net in 1968.

PINPOINTS

The history of a hockey team is made up of many smaller stories. These stories take place all over the map—not just in the city a team calls "home." Match the pushpins on these maps to the **TEAM FACTS**, and you will begin to see the story of the Bruins unfold!

1 Boston, Massachusetts—*The Bruins have played here since 1924.*

2 Flint, Michigan—*Tim Thomas was born here.*

3 Eveleth, Minnesota—*Frank Brimsek was born here.*

4 Comox, British Columbia—*Cam Neely was born here.*

5 Edmonton, Alberta—*Johnny Bucyk was born here.*

6 Dysart, Saskatchewan—*Fern Flaman was born here.*

7 Port Colborne, Ontario—*Bronco Horvath was born here.*

8 Montreal, Quebec—*Ray Bourque was born here.*

9 Birmingham, England—*Ken Hodge was born here.*

10 Trencin, Slovakia—*Zdeno Chara was born here.*

11 Villingen-Schwenningen, Germany—*Dennis Seidenberg was born here.*

12 Moscow, Russia—*Sergei Samsonov was born here.*

Bronco Horvath

GLOSSARY

AGILITY—Being quick and graceful.

ALL-STAR GAME—The annual game that features the best players from the NHL.

AMBUSH—Launch a surprise attack.

ART ROSS TROPHY—The annual award given to the NHL's top scorer.

ASSISTS—Passes that lead to a goal.

BACHELORS—Adult males who aren't married.

CONFERENCE—A large group of teams. There are two conferences in the NHL, and each season each conference sends a team to the Stanley Cup Finals.

DECADE—A period of 10 years; also specific periods, such as the 1950s.

DIVISION—A small group of teams in a conference. Each NHL conference has three divisions.

DRAFT—The annual meeting during which NHL teams pick the top high school, college, and international players.

DYNAMIC—Full of energy.

DYNASTY—A family, group, or team that maintains power over time.

EXECUTIVE—A person who makes important decisions for a company.

FEROCITY—Extreme intensity or fierceness.

FIRST-TEAM ALL-STAR—The annual award that recognizes the best NHL players at each position.

FORMULA—A set way of doing something.

HALL OF FAME—The museum in Toronto, Canada, where hockey's best players are honored. A player voted into the Hall of Fame is sometimes called a "Hall of Famer."

LEECHES—Wormlike creatures that feed by sucking blood.

LIMELIGHT—The focus of public attention.

LINE—The trio made up by a left wing, center, and right wing.

LOGO—A symbol or design that represents a company or team.

MASCOT—An animal or person believed to bring a group good luck.

MINOR LEAGUES—All the professional leagues that operate below the NHL.

MOST VALUABLE PLAYER (MVP)—The award given each year to the league's best player; also given to the best player in the playoffs and All-Star Game.

NATIONAL HOCKEY LEAGUE (NHL)—The professional league that has been operating since 1917.

OVERTIME—An extra period played when a game is tied after three periods. In the NHL playoffs, teams continue to play overtime periods until a goal is scored.

PLAYOFFS—The games played after the season to determine the league champion.

PLUS/MINUS RATING—A statistic that measures a player's effectiveness by comparing the goals scored for and against his team when he's on the ice.

ROOKIE—A player in his first year.

SHUTOUT—A game in which a team doesn't score a goal.

STANLEY CUP—The trophy presented to the NHL champion. The first Stanley Cup was awarded in 1893.

STANLEY CUP FINALS—The final playoff series that determines the winner of the Stanley Cup.

TRADITIONS—Beliefs or customs that are handed down from generation to generation.

UNSPECTACULAR—Ordinary or unremarkable.

VETERANS—Players with great experience.

LINE CHANGE

TEAM SPIRIT introduces a great way to stay up to date with your team! Visit our *LINE CHANGE* link and get connected to the latest and greatest updates. *LINE CHANGE* serves as a young reader's ticket to an exclusive web page—with more stories, fun facts, team records, and photos of the Bruins. Content is updated during and after each season. The *LINE CHANGE* feature also enables readers to send comments and letters to the author! Log onto:

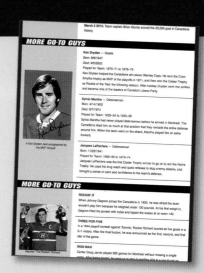

www.norwoodhousepress.com/library.aspx

and click on the tab: **TEAM SPIRIT** to access *LINE CHANGE*.

Read all the books in the series to learn more about professional sports. For a complete listing of the baseball, basketball, football, and hockey teams in the **TEAM SPIRIT** series, visit our website at:

www.norwoodhousepress.com/library.aspx

ON THE ROAD

BOSTON BRUINS
100 Legends Way
Boston, Massachusetts 02114
(617) 624-2327
http://bruins.nhl.com

HOCKEY HALL OF FAME
Brookfield Place
30 Yonge Street
Toronto, Ontario, Canada M5E 1X8
(416) 360-7765
http://www.hhof.com

ON THE BOOKSHELF

To learn more about the sport of hockey, look for these books at your library or bookstore:

* Cameron, Steve. *Hockey Hall of Fame Treasures.* Richmond Hill, Ontario, Canada: Firefly Books, 2011.

* MacDonald, James. *Hockey Skills: How to Play Like a Pro.* Berkeley Heights, New Jersey: Enslow Elementary, 2009.

* Keltie, Thomas. *Inside Hockey! The legends, facts, and feats that made the game.* Toronto, Ontario, Canada: Maple Tree Press, 2008.

INDEX

PAGE NUMBERS IN **BOLD** REFER TO ILLUSTRATIONS.

THE TEAM

MARK STEWART has written over 200 books for kids—and more than a dozen books on hockey, including a history of the Stanley Cup and an authorized biography of goalie Martin Brodeur. He grew up in New York City during the 1960s rooting for the Rangers, but has gotten to know a couple of New Jersey Devils, so he roots for a shootout when these teams play each other. Mark comes from a family of writers. His grandfather was Sunday Editor of *The New York Times*, and his mother was Articles Editor of *Ladies' Home Journal* and *McCall's*. Mark has profiled hundreds of athletes over the past 25 years. He has also written several books about his native New York and New Jersey, his home today. Mark is a graduate of Duke University, with a degree in history. He lives and works in a home overlooking Sandy Hook, New Jersey. You can contact Mark through the Norwood House Press website.

DENIS GIBBONS is a writer and editor with *The Hockey News* and a former newsletter editor of the Toronto-based Society for International Hockey Research (SIHR). He was a contributing writer to the publication *Kings of the Ice: A History of World Hockey* and has worked as chief hockey researcher at five Winter Olympics for the ABC, CBS, and NBC television networks. Denis also has worked as a researcher for the FOX Sports Network during the Stanley Cup playoffs. He resides in Burlington, Ontario, Canada with his wife Chris.